FURTHER PRAISE FOR

ANYBODY

"To speak any truth that can resonate beyond the particularities of their position, a poet must understand every particularity of that position, and all the forces that intersect to determine their view of the world. Banias is such a poet. It is questions about what constitutes the lyric and the universal . . . that drive his debut collection forward, and his readers into a more expansive, fully considered future." —*Fanzine*

"*Anybody* is a collection that pops and delights on first read, and then, under the lens of a second, expands and rewards. . . . Much of what *Anybody* succeeds at is seeing again and seeing better, which demands of us the very difficult and necessary human and social task of, first, looking beyond our seeing." —*Southeast Review*

"By putting on display his unruly thoughts, his random associations, his nagging worries, his shame, his lust, his tender hopes, [Banias] offers the reader an account of one person in the world, doing his best to make sense of the often senseless." —*Tikkun*

"Though Banias's poems are ever skeptical of static identity, gender, and privilege, he writes with a certainty of voice that inspires trust even as the locations of the poems stretch from the liminal to ignorable: cruising spaces, restrooms, a polluted lake, a surgical room for a double mastectomy." —*Publishers Weekly*

"I'm so impressed by the range and grace of Ari Banias's *Anybody*. It's discursive, straight-talking, and thinky, then ghostlike, elliptical, and mischievous. It takes its time, then rushes; it's quiet, then bold; it's steeped in sociality, then ringing with solitude. I happily recognize its arrival, even if I know (as does Banias, quoting Berlant) that recognition may be but the misrecognition we can bear." —Maggie Nelson

"Ari Banias is one of the best living poets, and this book in your hands is our proof. . . . This book *Anybody* is the courage of a poet who trusts the strength of poetry to make room in our world for everybody." —CAConrad

"Ari Banias has written one of the finest first books (OK, any book!) that I've ever read. . . . These poems stake a claim on the future: they give us a poet who understands to the bone how syntax and line and music embody emotion, and how the integrity of the spirit is the maker's integrity in going all the way to the bottom of these poems' large and important subjects." —Tom Sleigh

"Born late in the twentieth century, tutored under the twin suns of Frank O'Hara and Guillaume Apollinaire, vexed by 'this set of meanings on my body,' Ari Banias is a poet for this hour— bewildered, hopeful, and cracklingly alive, a citizen of the possible. *How many utopias*? (*keep imagining them*)." —Mark Doty

"Here is *Anybody* with its syntax of rupture and suture, its restless questions and metaphysical balloons. What a thrilling, original, generous, openhearted book. A book we have waited for, whoever we are."
                                                                                          —Donna Masini

ANYBODY

POEMS

ARI BANIAS

W. W. NORTON & COMPANY

INDEPENDENT PUBLISHERS SINCE 1923

NEW YORK | LONDON

For information about permission to reproduce selections from this book,
write to Permissions, W. W. Norton & Company, Inc.,
500 Fifth Avenue, New York, NY 10110

For information about special discounts for bulk purchases, please contact
W. W. Norton Special Sales at specialsales@wwnorton.com or 800-233-4830

Manufacturing by LSC Communications, Harrisonburg
Book design by JAM Design
Production manager: Louise Mattarelliano

Library of Congress Cataloging-in-Publication Data

Names: Banias, Ari, author.
Title: Anybody : poems / Ari Banias.
Description: First edition. | New York : W.W. Norton & Company, 2016.
Identifiers: LCCN 2016012493 | ISBN 9780393247794 (hardcover)
Classification: LCC PS3602.A6365 .A6 2016 | DDC 811/.6—dc23
LC record available at https://lccn.loc.gov/2016012493

ISBN 978-0-393-35544-4 pbk.

W. W. Norton & Company, Inc.
500 Fifth Avenue, New York, N.Y. 10110
www.wwnorton.com

W. W. Norton & Company Ltd.
15 Carlisle Street, London W1D 3BS

1 2 3 4 5 6 7 8 9 0

for Αργυρώ and Τριανταφιλλιώ

CONTENTS

ANYBODY

1

SOME KIND OF WE

These churchbells bong out
one to another in easy conversation
that wants to say
things are okay,
things are okay—
but things,
they are not okay, and I can't
trust a churchbell, though I would like to
the way I can trust
that in this country, in houses,
apartments, there somewhere is a cabinet or drawer
where it's stashed, the large plastic bag
with slightly smaller mashed-together
plastic bags inside; it is overflowing, and we keep adding,
bringing home more than we need, we should have
to weave a three-piece suit of plastic bags
a rug, a quilt, a bed of bags even, anything
more useful than this collection this excess
why am I writing about plastic bags, because
it is this year in this country and I am this person
with this set of meanings on my body and the majority of what I have,
I mean, what I literally
have the most of in my apartment, more than plants,
more than forks and spoons and knives combined, or chairs
or jars or pens or socks, is plastic bags, and I
am trying to write, generally and specifically,

through what I see and what I know,
about my life (about our lives?),
if in all this there can still be—tarnished,
problematic, and certainly uneven—a *we*.

AT ANY GIVEN MOMENT

Vito Corleone was a "strong" man, which is the main definition of a man
    I think.
At the table I say, smiling, I am weak. And everyone stares like,
why would you admit that?
        Because it's true.

So here I am
        in the hallway again. Chain motel. Nondescript corporate wallpaper
        of a beigey patterned variety. Gender, the room
I see myself walking into, all the rooms, any room, the number, the key

corresponding, and of course the whole
world's in there. Of course if I want to talk to almost *anyone*
        I have to go in!
It's too fucking small and we're all in it. But no, not all of you

seem to hate it. Here where all my dreams of showing up
to school in just underwear, flushed
before a windowsill of bean sprouts
nosing out of paper cups—I remember Eric suddenly,

the fourth grade outcast, in a freakout
pushing all the furniture around our classroom
in brilliant chaos. I didn't realize then the world
wouldn't fall apart if you did that. The corner of my desk

got jammed into my stomach
        which was startling but not personal.

What's personal is being here with all of you.

You know how you can't really look out a window without it
being a thing you're doing,
wistful or just framed in its way by you
being you and the window being a window? It isn't casual.

Everything is out there to be looked at and not to
look back at you who are small and like a god in your window.
One feels invisible then
                                    but we've definitely seen people

in the next building over in their underwear
on a bed watching TV in the heat. Multiple times.
The room where *we're* in our underwear watching TV is
      exceptionally small,
anyone would say so.

                    ▪

But bigger too in its way because the shades are drawn and though
we're beaded in a light sweat no one can see us,
we tell ourselves. Therefore the room is huge
and contains all we want to imagine. Given the heat
and that we are somewhat slower to think

in this humidity. Our near naked bodies in underwear we've decided

are outside that room. We are eternally outside, two
wildflowers in soil, faces upturned. The elements tend to us
gently with rain and light

but then of course large people in gloves come to poke
plastic tags into the soil
right beside us to help us be seen correctly

though we'd rather it all be
      a little less precise. I'm not *just* a flower.
At any given moment I'm also a weed and
medicinal and food for some bees and I don't know, just a thing
                    in the wind, a thing

in the ground. I like the feel, the sound
of that. But since I've imagined this room it must be
me who jabbed the tags into the soil.
With my blurry picture and beneath it

the scientific version of my name. I'm watching myself
watch TV in the heat in my underwear from the next building over, and
honestly, I seem overly angry.

      I think we should talk.   Can we all come to our windows?

NARRATIVE

For example, I was once
a sundress on a splintery
swingset in Texas, and the world
was made of yellow grass
struggling to live in sand, sand
beyond our fence, across the street,
sand that could have drowned us
but didn't. Because it was
a border town, there were other
others, so we sort of
belonged. The cacti, religiously
stoic, held promise, as did the mountains,
cast pink in the waning sun.
In Illinois I tried to build a kind of Midwestern
girlhood that failed and failed
into the shape of a flute
I played only high notes on.
I stopped eating
meat. Stopped speaking
Greek. Became an ear.
Now the only one I remember from that time
is the girl who looked like a boy or maybe
was one, who walked the same way home
I walked, same coat, same sneakers,
whom I never once greeted, just repeated
his-her name to myself: Dominick? Dominique?
Massively old trees canopied the cobbled streets.

The houses set so far apart you'd hear neither
argument nor song. Dominick.
Dominique. Not a stitch of recognition
passed between us.

WILDER,

Thank you for the drawing you sent (it looks like a dandy's hat with thoughts rushing into it) and for the photocopied passage about Agnes Martin & the self in art, gendered values of assertion vs. quietude, and where we expect to see what's deemed "political." Reading it improved my mood, which had been gloomy (and admittedly returned to a state of gloom again later), but that paragraph helped lift me briefly out of a despair I'd been living inside of with some irritating regularity. The kind of irritation that never quite naturalizes itself, which may be its best quality, how unwieldy yet somehow consistent it is, like counting on being the one guest in the large cardboard costume at an over-crowded party in a small sleek New York apartment. Yesterday while sitting on my floor I began looking deeply into the living room rug, an old rug that's new to me, and thought, I'd really like to disappear into this rug's dark blues and rusts and pinks, strange wobbly patterns that the more I look at them the more unsettlingly familiar they become, reflecting something both of this world and not, stiff flowering plants with geometric berries, robotic crabs wearing crowns, circuitry edged in spectral auras, coins on stems, spiders on crosses, pixelated like some crude early video game (only wool and warm and totally still), with four enormous blue ocean barges along its edge carting the rose-hued cargo of the soul—where to? Someplace. Terrific trees throughout laden with books and lamps and lumpy top hats, red bejeweled boots, droopy scep-ters, ghosts with bowtie eyes, wafer cookies on legs, alligator-faced roosters atop bronze trays . . . On either end of the rug a giant cat mae-stro presides (as "the man of the house" might at the head of a dining table), levitating two plump cherry bombs, aimed at the four enormous ocean barges (carrying our *souls!*) which most of the time I don't give consideration to and so step on daily.

ON POCKETS

I told you to write a poem about pockets
but you already wrote a paper on pockets in Dickens
and I have read almost no Dickens to be honest but pockets
what a staple of intimate transport both private and exposed
functional and decorative some faux ones even printed on
others in women's clothes hold nearly nothing
intrigue me deeply they have so many ways of being
prominent or discreet or altogether hidden
buttoned snapped zippered flapped but then also those
on fine suit jackets one has to slit the first time with a blade
the care of that and how sexual it is but this isn't what's
important about pockets pockets are dreams of negative
space and possibilities potentials secret inside-outside places a pocket
of thinking a pocket of resistance theoretical and cultural
writings on pockets exist but as with Dickens I neglect them
when it comes to pockets I prefer to think on my own
I still at times imagine my thoughts
in a small enclosure it helps me think better
when actually I have a mind full of holes they breathe
there's something sweet and forlorn about a pocket
breached a torn pocket a pocket that can't
hold what's important its one job a keeper
and through the compromised place things escape
down a pant leg or into the lining of a coat if it's cold out
one can feel a warm coin pass along the leg against the skin maybe
hear metal strike sidewalk but not always, not always coins, maybe keys,
if dropped on carpet or in a loud place not heard, or not a hole

but a pickpocket, wind, carelessness, somewhere crowded
when going through their contents in a hurry
more and more of mine have holes as I get older
I'm too lazy to repair or notice only when wearing this parka,
these pants, and picture when I get home
the needle and thread in the drawer and then get home
where my pockets no longer exist their relevance declines I forget
today I saw an old friend in a strange yet handsome dark wool coat
    that struck me
I couldn't say why, its eerie beauty
and I told him so, he said there are no pockets it's a prisoner's coat

GIANT SNOWBALLS

All winter two giant snowballs stood in the center
of the trampled schoolyard, & another one
off to the side I felt foolish
feeling bad for. Every day
I observed them through the chainlink fence.

Three giant snowballs the strewn
parts of a would-be snowperson's body.
I'm trying not to say "snowman"
but we know. He's blank
and numb and separated
so much from himself. The segments of him
roughly equal in size: his head and his trunk and
the lower ball I won't call legs.

Yesterday it snowed,
so today the kids build new ones
all different sizes & blindingly white.
On the sides where the sun doesn't shine,
shadows fall, light blue and uncomplicated.

Beside the largest snowball
rests a much smaller one, and I can't help
but see them as mother and child
& wow what a stupid human cultural mess.

Now there are six snowballs and I miss
my old loneliness.

WHO YOU'RE ABOUT TO BE

This new boy's trying not to be another version of the boy
who chewed, rearranged, and then put back your insides.

And he's not. He has different eyes, a gentler voice, a sweeter grin.
And he's much more terrifying.

I try to shrug it off,
but sometimes I look at him
and for a second he has that other boy's face on.

In a way, every boy's the boy who chewed out your insides.
Every girl is either the boy, or your mother.

So where's the man with the large chin who was your father?
I always look for him near New Jersey.

I haven't yet realized that with various sorts of chins,
in various places inside and out of the U.S.,
he is everywhere; how many replicas there can be of a father.

When will I realize that a boy who chewed out someone's insides
became my father, or that I could one day become
my father, chew out someone's insides, probably my own.

But the boy, what gets you about the boy
is that he looks at you with such tenderness, and nesting in the
    tenderness,

with a small clicking sound like a minute hand or teeth,
a desire to devour you.

You've looked at a person that way yourself, with nothing
ticking in your throat but hunger.

You've looked and wanted to take everything sweet
without having to know. Said you did want to know but actually,
not wanted to.

When you think you see what looks like it
ignite, flare its matchlight over his face—

when it calls to you across such a short space, a couple feet
of mattress, a few inches of air, the time it takes
to get to the door, be down the stairs, run

down the buckling sidewalks
without tripping as fast as you can—you're there,
ripping into a hard sprint, gone, gone

but still with him in that bed, the both of you

slowly then quickly then slowly becoming
the feared and wanted ones.

GRANDCHILD

She says so the aunt and uncle and cousins all look
in unison ooooh their approval
What a beautiful girl while we hunch
on the veranda in jeans and baggy t-shirt not

what she means by beauty hardly
a girl our hair barber-cut
five years our chest inside two sports bras flattened
further by the fabric bandage we pin close

around our torso adamant
inside of awkward gesture-awkward awkward
to speak dodging pronouns to visit to sleep
on the lace-draped living room couch

so visible to all avoiding
awkward trips to the sea with cousins
who act like nothing's changed only sitting
beside *yiayia* when she says

our name and pats the cushion deliberately
draws our hand into her shaking ones and puts
on us the same ring that engaged her
to him at sixteen she says

It will be time to start a family soon
looking at our face touching the bristle of our hair
saying Beautiful you are
the only one who has my name

AN ARROW

Too often I'd like some direction
but am ashamed of this fact, still I ask for it
though men are supposed be bad at admitting
they're lost, why men agree
to fulfill this is lost on me.
Who cares what men are. Can't we
scrap this whole enterprise,
top-down management
small talk, normative dating. A little box
I fill in over and over, like feeding pennies into a slot
it leads somewhere I think
I'm saving them. For when? The dropdown menus reach
longer and longer, so to scroll becomes
the new version of a sweeping gesture, more ways
to be erased. At the end of the day
we still march on directionless,
used by pronouns & all the livelong
language still drags us through its shitty toll plazas,
do "you" have a highway phobia like "I" do.
Or who do you feel most related to. Under my breath I say Love
thy neighbor as thy self
is to thy as neighbor is to the scraggle
in my front yard is to a badly pruned bush
across the street. But love it & those neighbors
drunk and too loud on their porch while I'm trying to sleep
to love us all better. The steepest hill
in maybe all of Oakland California,

walking up it leg muscles burning, love the fortune
to have legs the cinderblock the succulent and none of them equal,
fuck equality, predicated on sameness
why not by now insist on a complex star cluster
a fuck of will and willingness and imagination, our most unwieldy
crap? But crap, I'm daily losing my grip as if having
handed my only bow and arrow to a stranger who
might shoot it off look at that thing! it could hit
someone I care about or love, you myself anyone or a bush
here's another bush and another they all mash together,
one is pine-ish the other has purple flowers, it's basically formless
& somehow I feel it's my key relative
that cousin I'm always close to no matter how many years pass,
who once cared about art now he's a depressed socialist
vaguely entrepreneurial by necessity, as once I was
a slutty teenage girl they now call Sir, I guess I can see that
here's another bush that could be shaped into another form
or just left alone. Outside the neighbor kids
shout without regard like their parents
before them, I saw one kid the other day point a phone
from their window into mine to take a photo of me I wanted to take
one in response as reminder that hey it's a window
not a mirror and the object talks back

SOLVE FOR X

if there was a word for it.
when pushing down reason.
if more than a boy.
if shaking took care of it.
if cured by looking.
if no lemon juice to lighten the hair.
if another girl could step out of you, a shared one.
if her face was loosened by salt.
if home was unjustly sunlight.
when the other way around was a mountain.
if light curtained it.
if it dodged windows.
if maybe is the only thing enormous.
if less than a boy is a fruit.
villages of light were pushed down inside you.
a sea of anotherness.
when the pronoun curtain.
if a ring undoes the hand.
when a zipper becomes impossible.
a curtain behind the curtain.
if girl is less than lace.
if barely can pass for maybe.
if boy was covered in possible light.
if she stiffens when praised.
when salt was sung.
and a face was just a face.
if he bristles always at the name.

if nostalgia is a type of blue light.
maybe could still be beautiful.
if right now is bandaged.
when even what didn't happen happened.

CLOSE

The book I almost finished.
The look I gave you
while you weren't looking and now
you'll never know the way I feel.
Oh well. Most paint jobs
are shoddy. I wrote "pain jobs"
then fixed it. On my desk three stones
two earplugs and a tangerine.
The earplugs and tangerine resemble
each other in color, but this doesn't
hugely matter. If only we didn't
care about what doesn't matter
but people do. An awful TV show where
women fight in reality over something
unreal: a "good man." I say
unreal but mean invented. I consult
the bat necklace hanging above
my desk when angry, a talisman
of decentralized personal power.
You've given me a bad name
I'll only make worse.
I collect stones because
they won't leave me before
I leave this world. By night,
trees that in daylight look dark
transform to beige
oversized insect legs flailing in a garden
that's mostly a shitty

walkway between buildings
city dwellers would covet a view of
because it's better than no window.
Better than nothing: I wouldn't say that
of the "good man" who fucked
with "unparalleled enthusiasm" last summer
but I'd say it of you.

ONE POSSIBLE READING AMONG MANY

A person can learn to live
under various sorts of conditions.

This current room features furniture
for resting and furniture for eating
pushed as far apart as possible to give
the feel of two distinct spaces,

opposing sides like lovers' backs
turned mute in sleep or argument—

soured but determined, its whole arrangement
a stubbornness.

I see myself right now sitting at a desk, and ten years from now
sitting at a desk, and in between

climbing a parched hill wild with thyme,
fucking strangers who stay strangers and others
                    who won't, and feeling bored the way
I felt bored as a child, boundlessly, as if boredom were a disease
that touched everything the eye did.

Today the books on the table lie shut.
I've stacked them
like a row of class portraits in which
one after the next the faces perform what they have learned, or
     they try very much

not to perform it. To learn to see beyond my seeing
I need to admit everything.

VILLAGERS

boxes taped up and up then tied with twine | addressed on every side | in that careful longhand taught on other continents | they looked like mail bombs | going round and round the carousel | in a regional anxiety | stinking barrel of sheep's cheese beaded in sweat | olive oil tin wrapped in much plastic | each printed letter a rounded separate bundle | standing on its own | the sore thumbs of my parents' immigrant luggage at the United terminal | a friend who doesn't speak at airports | except when spoken to | word for home that could also mean journey | or never-arrived | at the baggage claim | a person waits in a t-shirt printed with English words | whose arrangement is nonsensical | and it doesn't matter | that what matters is far | while right here at any moment— | no one need remind anyone | tether that | suitcases duffels packages | taped and bound so emphatically they look like total crap | what matters is the words are undeniably English | anyone can tell you this | is why the shirt exists | tether that to this | anyone whose intimate particular knowledge lives | with a line drawn through it | "they were a simple people" | my mother often said | from whom she untethers | and bundles into packages | all taut with twine and sends away | at the carousel on which they circulate | printed with her surname | she could | and might refuse them | that "they were a simple—" | was the sort of thing that sparked in me a rage | which I am only now beginning to draw a line through | line I wish to repeople myself | on the other side of | with a friend | a dear friend | who | doesn't speak at airports unless spoken to

MORPHOLOGY

I stood, a cloud of hair, teased up & sprayed in place, distinct
from the surrounding air. Somebody wore me on her head,

took orders. Withstood me

held and measured as a breath. Halo-gold, they said
I fixed her to the ground.

A fist and spoon they
kissed this into shape: say *me*, say *mine*, see *I*

as senator and its constituents.
My freedoms stirred until they turned constraints.

In mirrors, I eyed me;
in storefront glass, in lakes. Touched tip of *I* to tip
to make a loop. This way, I felt both long and bunched. I felt like guts

some vultures who were me tore at.

I stood against a wall, under consideration, a paint chip
taped there, half-unseen;

and leaning in prairie where wind combed & petted the tooth of me.

Some called I *she*, or *he* (or *it* or *they*).

Some taught me famous names, to drop the coins of these
in slots of conversation so with others I might feel like we.

But *I* at the shore of a sea, *I* on the pebbled, tar-smeared edge
of an island. There hungered or grumbled or stood an astonished *I*
I picked at like a splinter once part of something bigger.

These patches of dwindling snow, undifferentiated, but shapely.
Their yellow spots where something stood & peed.
And that admitting earth beneath.

DOUBLE MASTECTOMY

Comprehend it?—

the creaking house we lived in,
that hundred-year-old matron

the new owners razed—   how could I,
how could they.

The curved banister, the glass knobs
where were these now—

                                    some dump?

Could be made of these parts

Frankenstein   —home?

        ■

Glided straight toward that white
room. As if

approaching from within
a dense wood

a place queerly brimming   gold light;
the possibility of

        the possibility of

my body.

THE FLATTENED GRASS THAT HOLDS
YOUR SHAPE

So it turns out there is no clearing with sunlight and trumpets.
There is the grimy windowsill with its paint-cracked lip.
The refrigerator seeming to ready itself
for some moment when it will finally act. And the misery
of neighbors whose lives only touch
your life in this way: get the fuck out & don't you dare & I swear
to God just you try. There is
no galloping triumph, righteous and purposed. No fatherly shield.
There is electricity and heat. Garish overhead lighting.
Four plates, two cups, three bowls. There are things to eat.
And salt on the sidewalks so now there is salt on the floor.
The freight train's whistle of come and go.
No rebellion, no longing, no unswept bundle
of flotsam and dust resembling the smallest tender nest.
No doorbell, but some days mail. Bills and ads mostly.
There's a tree across the schoolyard, a giant
whose branches fan out with such greed
and this greed an unabashed gluttony for air.
More often, there are dull words because the interesting ones
are elsewhere. There are pencils, a damp dishtowel, dry skin.
There is no toilet paper again. There is no cathartic shouting then
storming off into the night or the morning, no slapped cheek,
shaken shoulders, no spilled wine blossoming into a purple
stain. There is a scavenged lamp whose shade, way oversized and
partly discolored, recalls a thrift store t-shirt bought by mistake.
There is cleverness in small bursts. There is what one hopes for

and then buries out of cowardice. There is cowardice
that enters a person and grows. There are pot-of-gold promises.
The dolled-up pet store owner
and the older butch who works there
she treats like a dog. A half-desperate dog one begrudgingly pets.
There's not really forgiveness, nor certainty, nor rescue, nor rest, nor
any signal that it will be the last kiss. There are eyebrows,
such libraries of expression. There's a park
plush and generous like the mother of everyone, and like anyone
with a mother can, they all take it for granted. There are bicycles
    and there is snow
and there's the strange act of riding out into the snow.

THE MEN

Fire Island Pines

It seems necessary to say I watch them.
It seems necessary: *them*. This distance
between us. How at times it can shrink, then grow

with the removal of clothing.
Proximity.

From here, it seems necessary to say I didn't.
Join or belong but

there where mouth meets
crotch, I did

want to, I did. Walk along the paths,
part marsh, part dune,
exchange glances.

Someone said
how old are you but I didn't
answer him. He's still vivid

in only a cowboy hat
combat boots & trunks

Follow him:
grey t-shirt, baseball hat, blue eyes.

Shoulders burnt by unending noon
he places his hands on while
he works on him, a kindness.

Someone says take out your dick,
I want to see it.

I lose him
on a forking path.

I'm standing some yards behind the men
who watch the men; we're watching us

pose
ass-up on a blanket.

"A boy's a man
who can't get hard."

Prowl daily
in only a towel.

Suppose I could, I can.

Find a way
of walking into their *us*

the sound of their pleasures. As though
it were an ocean.

Find a different
spot where we
do our thing. We two

who are alike.
A few crouch to look but

we're positioned just so

no one sees exactly,
though one could imagine

a hole is a hole is a hole is a hole—

fanning out to the nameless
late afternoon—

what isn't there. Isn't there
a sweetness to that.

We is something like a cloud. How big, how thick,
its shape—ambiguous. We is moving across
a magnificent sky. We see the sky all around us but
also, we can look down at our own hands.
A cloud is a changing thing. Sometimes we are an animal
smiling, clawing at something
not there. Other times we spread out so thin we almost
don't exist. We are thickening just now. A sea of slow
knitting. And soon it will rain, and we
will be down in the grass again.
A blade of grass gets thirsty;
it's nice to think we could quench that.
It's something we might really be good at. But then
arms get in the way,
remind us we're separate. Lying side by side
and looking into another pair of eyes as if
there's a way to see into the dark
pupil's pit, some place "beyond."
Other times whose hands are whose,
our mouths together the permeable
entrance to the bright underworld chamber,
and a rush of remembering
all eyes are lit from behind, the wiring rigged back to the same
source, like putting together so many
small things you have a better, bigger thing.
Relative to what? It doesn't matter.
There's something to be said for individuality,
multiplied. The earth is breathing out through countless eyes

asking every possible ray of light to meet every possible rainstorm.
They do attract. And aloneness only keeps getting bigger.
One day we will tell all about it. At our own table.
There are things we cannot see. Most things. Most of all.

2

EXQUISITE CORPSE

I had a nightgown once, which
became a jellyfish

so in order to wear it I had to go down:
to punch myself into the form

the content required,
to hunker like a boulder under

immeasurable pressure, as when
minerals are transformed

into their reverse.
As when a nightgown is worn
over the tuxedo for years.

Pissing on a jellyfish sting
is said to make one
feel normal or royal.

When we were together
in the house by the sea,

there was still a sea. Before
being set adrift,

tuxedo and nightgown
lay slain, ashore where
the surf inched up and up and if

lapels say a word then burn her
down to a pair of molten cufflinks
they piss on till normal.

It is expected
he kiss her and become a nightgown.

She wears him
in order to punch him down

until he sinks, until it's said he is
painless as a house

or some comparable
soft-bodied animal that drifts.

THE FEELING

Each spring, a cloud travels up from the south
to an island in the Aegean.
The red cloud is coming, the townspeople say.
Or, the red cloud has been here.
What cloud? my mother asks. Since when?
The red cloud covers the buildings, the cars,
in a fine red film of dust from elsewhere.
That we imagine we cannot feel the wars
is an American feeling. That we cannot see them,
they are somewhere else.
But someone pays the police. We do.
That we are meant to believe the poem can say moon
but not government. Both have flags
attached and can make a body
howl beyond its will. They punctuate existence
even if I believe I can't feel them;
they legislate, they leak.
The moon which is always here
even if it cannot be seen. The inmates
and the detainees in correctional facilities and jails and prisons,
in maximum and minimum, in solitary
cannot see the moon, or they can.
The inmates who are here, always,
even if I cannot see them, who cannot speak to me
or who do, but am I listening? Are we listening,
to poems? Not much.
Therefore I can say anything. No;
I can say moon and tree and fox and river,

or me and you, or love and stutter,
but I can mean corporation I can mean police.
I can mean surveillance,
or that the moon is a prison, it is daytime,
and in daytime nearly no one sees the moon.
And the tree is a television
where the president appears in the form of a finch.
He sings gorgeously; people swoon.
We learn that finches eat mostly seeds
small and harmless, so when the tree flowers
in spring we forget the moon
and its mute armaments. How drunk we become
on blossoms. We don't ask
what kind of seeds or where they're from.
We hum along with the finches, with the sirens, with the rivers,
with the police; a harmony whose falling droplets
we can't feel. And meanwhile,
a law ushered through noiselessly, mandating seeds.
This is not our poem. The poem has been privatized.
Its flag will be a red feeling.

PRAIRIE RESTORATION PROJECT

The Midwest is a huge flat kitchen table I'm sitting at,
drinking rusty water, looking at a huge flat field
out the window. The field's the actual
size of loneliness, emptied of people.
With my looking, I try to gather

its birds picking at some seeded thing, its combed
pattern of plow-strokes, the gravel on a road
dividing field from field, to pull them all in close
against the way looking at it feels

like a dispersal. With my mind I roll the fragments
between thumb and forefinger, every
jagged edge and ridge, each smooth lip,
scallop, curve, nondescript
pebbles upon pebbles of it. Loneliness

whose sheep I gather from pasture,
herding them now into a very small pen. Always, one
is missing, or I lost count, counted wrong, never knew
how many we started off with.
What's that called, at the beginning—
whatever grew in the field or grazed there.
How we blink and chew and find ourselves

cubicle-hunched, tightened under humming fluorescents,
shrinking down in rented mud. Dutifully visiting
the raised square of dirt someone called garden, poking it

with little heart, having signed the shitty contract
for the dim apartment where the appliances
only half-work, and each passing night
breaks their backs further. I counted wrong.
I remember what a mountain was

was dry macaroni glued to a sheet of paper
in a kitchen in the later part of the last century. I picked
the pieces off each by each in boredom or nervousness;
they ticked dryly against the side of a paper cup.
How many fields like this there are ahead of us,
blue with the absence of tallgrass.

TO THE GOD OF SOBRIETY

I've got to get as far away as possible

from what I know

If that's you doing it

keep unplugging the world

Invite me softly around the back

Show me the jumble

of wires & switches

the piling-up junk drawer:

toothpicks rubber bands

soy sauce packets pennies rumpled napkins

those twisty-ties their future lives!

How could I turn back?

I've got to get as far away as possible

from what I know

Make it so I can't *not* knock

the frame that's always hung there

off the wall

& find the punched-in hole

HANDSHAKE

Now I'm a fake man I'm talking moving but
I never learned how.   I'm faking and not-faking it, making it
up as I go which so far means
I don't know what's expected & I'm probably not doing it right
hell, I don't care—
a handshake is awkward   a hug is too

The choices: cheating husband, vapid fag
checked-out corporate guy, self-centered evolved guy, sensitive
yet inarticulate, predator, messiah, martyr, angry man, father
god-awful! & I would like ethics to play a role but
is compelling fashion too much to ask for?

I'm not sure I want to do this but here goes
drop my pants and the needle sinks in. Is it weird I feel it surge
powerfully through me? OK maybe that's imaginary

but not the question of what it means to be a white dude
                                                after having been a white girl—
How much is learned how much given how much taken on voluntarily?

I know I'd prefer to misbehave
continuously. Any squirrel gets what I mean—anarchic revelry,
refusing to ever be still, such keenness.
They own no tree so they all own all of them.
I'd like to flick my tail too whenever I want as if to say WHAT.

But at any moment I'm wherever someone puts me—

then change my mind. I'll pick a side
when I need to

       handshake: OK;   backslap-chortle: no way.

■

Sometimes we're engulfed by sides.

Granted this is no place to air-kiss or shake hands
but I'm pleased to meet you however I can.

This page another frame like any   you look through & are

invited to step into
And though I've never
met your body before and you've never met mine I am sure
they are spinning out someplace past where anyone could reach
I am sure now
there is no true body

our cells are always still freaking out.

When I went on vacation with my dad
it was awkward. Were we two men sharing a bed. Were we father
and daughter. We fought
as we often have, like brothers.

At dusk we took a walk into town.
You know what we call this? he said.
Wolf-light. Just after sundown the sky a deep bruise
the air anticipates.

A SUNSET

I watch a woman take a photo
of a flowering tree with her phone.
A future where no one will look at it,
perpetual trembling which wasn't
and isn't. I have taken photos of a sunset.
In person, "wow" "beautiful"
but the picture can only be
as interesting as a word repeated until emptied.
I think I believe this.
Sunset the word holds more than a photo could.
Since it announces the sun then puts it away.
We went to the poppy preserve
where the poppies were few but generous clumps
of them grew right outside the fence
like a slightly cruel lesson.
I watched your face, just out of reach.
The flowers are diminished by the lens.
The woman tries and tries to make it right
bending her knees, tilting back.
I take a photo of a sunset, with flash.
I who think I have something
to learn from anything learned nothing from the streetlight
that shines obnoxiously into my bedroom.
This is my photo of a tree in bloom.
A thought unfolding
across somebody's face.

YOUR WILD DOMESTICATED INNER LIFE

Experience is a lamb. Memory
leads that lamb by a rope
uphill again to the rocky plot of land
where your ancestors once farmed.
Every time you set out
the lamb resists, pulls a steady NO
against the rope. Does it know
something you don't? You know the trees are up there
waiting for you—and the orchards!—the vineyards!
But it keeps pulling; it's a lamb. Stout and gentle and stubborn.
And our own lives always seem ordinary to us.
When your father was a boy
an actual pet lamb slept on his head every night.
This wasn't remarkable then but the family
likes to tell the story like look how far we've come.
They skip the part about him
setting cats on fire. Now he's a doctor with a sleek
apartment. Nothing chipped or old or broken
in it. There's no way to take a picture
of how it feels; it doesn't
feel a thing. Meanwhile, olive trees continue
striking tragic poses in the Greek countryside
as if for the first time—how can they stand it?
How can it be that the path
you and the lamb
have worn into the mountain
is, for the lamb, new every time? The collapsed walls
of the farmhouse swallowing themselves.

A prim chorus the almond grove. Every time!
Or could it be the lamb that's new?
At the end of a rope, all lambs act the same.
If you're their shepherd maybe they are telling you to be alive
is to pull against something
far stronger than you. So don't be
a damn doctor about it. Maybe it's time
to be the little black hooves in mountain dirt,
a body tethered to another
body to this earth.

WHERE WE SIT WATCHING

Even if rearranged not to look like a story, everything
is; some heist, some Buick weaving down the highway
with a lacy froth of squad cars floating behind it
like the train behind a wedding gown

There is a small boy somewhere carrying those squad cars
he rehearsed it, all ceremonious
inside the television very small wearing a bowtie & sweating lightly
        one sock bunches in his shoe the seam pressing red
against his pinkie toe but he mustn't stop, he must
do this work of lifting up the train,
because the bride is important and the boy so small
he cannot be seen, even if you get so close to the screen
the pixels split

                into red and green and blue
miniature Chiclets stacked on top of each other,
this boy somewhere inside
walking slow keeping three
inches between each footstep as he's been instructed,
so the bride can dazzle as if no one were ever there
to lift anything slightly related to her, the train
follows her silver-white, the troopers
all spangle their sirens hypnotic we forget
she's a fugitive so caught up are we
in the spectacle of the procession and that dress
engulfing her like a diamond does its beholder

And the boy so small he is unseeable
cannot scratch the itch on his ankle
cannot let go this train or look anyplace
        but ahead, to keep pace with his bride
he mustn't pause, drag a foot, or hurry
the train must not crinkle, or fold or bend or be taut or pull at all
but should move with liquid grace
that communicates ease, a spill or breeze
through salon-styled hair

So that when we watch we forget her dress
is the car, we forget the story though the story's
the reason we're gripped, but if we start to ask why
this should matter so much our bride shudders right then
        & we're swallowed
by her and the boy and the dress and
our half-formed question is lost, we see only

the meaningful walk over cold marble, we join
the rows & rows of congregation beaming up
like scenery along a highway, mute and unimportant, cars,
    billboards,
half-landscaped roadside—but sometimes a rush
of small purple flowers; and other times just shrubs,
        though who designed them? I would like to know the person
who decided *here there will be shrubs, shrubs*
will definitely be best along this exit

                     where the bride will one day
veer off and attempt escape for good but where
they'll run her into a cul-de-sac and surround
her like a pack of foaming dogs, a jeweled
tidal wave she'd all that time
been just one step ahead of
and the rosebushes will be in bloom soft as earlobes and she
     will stoop
to put her face in one as a small boy holds our breath

WEDDING

People, far too many people here—
drinking, leaning on the furniture,
congratulating my father
on his new life. Here's
his young wife, young enough
to be my older sister.
She—if you can't tell
the whole truth—is *nice*.
But he slams his glass
onto the table, yells
more now than ever. Unless
I remember wrong. I know
I was afraid. Of him. And so.
I know I played alone
with dolls and that
we roughhoused, hard,
like brothers. What is a father
is a question like what
is home, or love. In the middle of the room
guests on the arms of the awful floral sofa
Mom wouldn't get up from
when she heard. In the grey bathrobe
for a week, horrid splotches
of pink and purple flowers with green
for stems. Or leaves. I can't
look at it. There's something hot
behind my eyes another glass of wine
should take care of.
There are people I should say hello to.

ENOUGH

Even here in this highway rest stop
I could meet the hottest person of my dreams
which could be anyone, and if meant to be
they won't be repelled by what wafts off me
though the notion I have to be ready
with choice wit like a blurb for my soul repels me,

and other times just the assumption my beloved is white,
the idea of white people loving each other at all
when in whiteness together we steamroll what matters,
that *we* a fake universal I've wanted to wreck
by how I live, if we look at it hard enough
would we actually still love each other? I feel sick.

What may seem here a sudden tonal swerve or shift
in subject is one I'm confident the poem can recover from,
and anyway I'm out to argue
it's no shift at all but rather a necessary widening of scope.
This rest stop in question brims with white people
of which I am yet another, and therefore am I to feel safe or at home

because honestly, prior to using the men's room I bristle
at the idea of who in it might threaten me,
but hey the body calls
loudly and so far I have come and gone each time
unscathed which, like most violence or its absence,
is not random. As inherently two anybodies

feeling affection fondness affinity or yes love
is not in itself a trouble, though it often & plainly to various others
a trouble has meant and become,
any unquestioned allegiance deemed natural is to me
cause for alarm, so I want to say something
difficult and disarming here, as if the saying itself were enough

to unhinge us all from the behemoth
except nothing comes to mind, only how the sight
of a straight couple stumbling into a queer bar to make out
in one of its holy gritty corners for thrills
spawns in me an ancient rage from the floor of my gut a million
cells in me turning to face out sputtering fire

but really, one couple's specific affection can't be
the true origin of my rage, that ember
lies daily inside me in wait by the minute to alight or turn
toward any seemingly deserving targets of which they appear to be one.
If I were a person far larger perhaps braver I would lift them
by the scruffs of their necks like kittens

who moments from now will forget this,
and say scram will you the rest of the world's
already yours while flinging them not altogether gently off.
But I am not that person. I'm who, clenching, fumes as when
I think about white people, for instance myself
and a friend, or a lover, or me and a family member loving each other

as much as we do and what this means in the world I fume
so intensely I often grow sick with the image of us.
My mother would be greatly upset by this.
When a white acquaintance asks where in the city I live and
is the neighborhood safe, she means such
a clutch of what she won't admit to meaning but

weeds push up through such poorly concealed cracks
and I salute their rogue stubborn raggedy green,
what persistence, though some days I'm sorry for the sidewalks too,
that countless human feet fall on until beyond repair
they crack and I ask myself under the attention of what
large abstracted force concentrated
into a singular point of pressure will I too someday come apart

WHO IS GHOST

who is ghost, the translucent almost
who flotilla, is footless
is died and come back, who sheet
and *oooo* is remembered

is ghost is flicking
on and off the lights is brush
the shoulder with gauzy touch
who is whisper in ear whisper
of curtain in and out with breeze who
flash is haze is gone

forgotten is ghost
the ones with different names now
the girl they say became a _____ who is he
who one time got kissed in a field
it was summer bare ankles dampened by night grass
who was uncurled is shook out

the candle with four matches sunk in its wax
who any flame is

      is the prairie taken by it
the half-made bed the half-said word
before it folds up into the throat

the first time someone took off your clothes
the clothes themselves
      is ghost

A VERSION

of course, we go to smoke: girls' bathroom, music wing
duck the last locked stall

where no toilet, instead a little half-door
secret passage into the wall

       inside-inside, pressed so close the odd warp of piano
tentative violin notes mustered in airless rooms

ash, brickdust, my small practiced cough
then sneaking out before the bell. wooden smell of old chairs,

unseen inner plush
of clarinet cases, dull

posters no one looks at
but look: my one power here

is long straight hair, the silk
that lets me glide instead of stumble—like that,

impossible: the always wincing strange body
with the face glowing for show, encoded

further down than the thing
       folded, passed from jeans pocket

              to jeans pocket, intimate, privileged
information: you know: the other self is strangled,

spangled, glossed &
smothered.

                    but somewhere keeping score: the weird quiet

kid smashing bottles by the underpass

                                  & outlasts this

AREN'T WE

Aren't we so in on it together. Don't we
hurt. Like huge holes in the ground
where demolished brick buildings stood
where weeds momentarily thrive
glass-faced condos will rise
soon don't we hurt. At future
cocktail parties in those buildings aren't we
attending uncomfortably, but not
so uncomfortably we don't know people
who bought in the building. This was years
from now. But we hurt don't we, brightly.
Zoned in where the pits dug out
by floodlight make sleep hard to come by.
For who when glass or brick hurts
hardest has to move. Now move
along. Near the park on the block
where the coffee is suddenly strong. Not what I
call an accident. The vinyl awnings
swapped for distressed wood signs. We did that.
We would. What did
the before-buildings look like one could ask
but nostalgia seems novice.
Or as if we make claims beyond our so modest
brightness. So many choices at the bodega
now called a market.
In the future don't we excel at
confusing ourselves about an experiment
in success that becomes actual hurt

made culture. Made rich
by scholarly interventions
into public loss. And oh I suppose
we meant to do that didn't we. That sort of accident

GAY BARS

| Best Friends Club | Hideaway | Chameleons | Just Us |

Somewhere in Time | There | The Edge | Nevermore

| Someplace Else | The Other Place | Utopia | Cell Block |

The Other Side | My Sister's Room | Crossroads | Sugar Shack

| Lion's Den | Stage Door | Maneuvers | Questions |

Tramps | Legends | Brothers | The Flame

| One Love | After Dark | Heads Up | Panic |

Buddies | Innuendo | In Between | Out of Bounds

| Backstreet | Masque | Wild Card | The Odds |

Club Detour | Vice Versa | Outskirts | Above and Beyond

| Uncle Elizabeth's | Five Cent Decision | Chances R | The Park |

The Right Corner | Paradise Inn | Temptations | The Trapp

| Bambi's Bottoms Up | Manhole | Charmers | Blendz |

Alias | Alibi's | The Backdoor | Faces

| Touché | Temple | Nutbush | Club Try |

Monkey Business | The Closet | Hush on Congress | Why Not III

| Bubby and Sissy's | Drama Club | Different Seasons | Oz |

The Eagle | SideKicks | A Man's World | 'Bout Time

| Equals | Exhale | Esquire | Exile |

R House | Ain't Nobody's Business | Heaven | Crazy Fox

HOG

My heart is a hog riding solo,
highway hot, wind-smeared, ripping alongside a field,
so famished it would eat your corsage.
You're a fawn in the field,
flickering there inquisitively. A startled, tawny thing,
self-protective, liable to leave. No, I'm the fawn, quite hungry.
The field is you, and I'm not sure. What's a hog
but gleam of handlebars, leather, that roar speeding by.
The scared parts dressed up tough, saying
ah come on let's go chop up the wind.
But the hog-part of me knows how easy
scaring comes: we are small brave clouds in a large thunder show.
The body used to be everything—
every skin-prick, every sympathy. Remember?
How our ears twitched.
And now the field, a meadow of light green,
uniform to the eye, where all along the ground,
other sympathies, ecstatic, buried, reinvent love.
A world barely visible & therefore alive.
At any moment the field could bloom, stadium-huge.
I keep roaring past, circling back.
There's something you should know about me, you said.
A motor started up vaguely behind us, a water tank,
a truck backing up with drawled-out beeps, a coughing motorbike.
Mint stood at attention in the garden but no one saw it
because the moon was new, meaning, invisible.
There's something you should know about me, I said.
Your body flexed like a field under a herd of cattle,

who can feel it through their hooves, their lips
against the field's coarse grass,
who don't ask does the ground hold them up
or do they pin it down. They don't flinch
when my engine cuts and instinct
dismounts, stupid
engine, idiot love. We stand chewing, dust clouded.
Cattle about to be over,
field that blinks what. what. what. what.

3

BOUQUET

Today I build flowers out of concepts
in order to speak to you sincerely.
Today you want nothing because wanting
comes too close to feeling.
And though a sad old person
who combs their silver hair
all afternoon in a high window
curses you with great acuity,
you being anyone in a suit, a suit
being whatever you insulate yourself with
so you don't hear that voice up there
calling you out, you keep going
as grim fleets of semis keep going,
shuttling dry goods across the continent.
In their fervent rumble lives
a hope to be getting paid soon. I get it.
Even last night's cream roses still in their cellophane
and chucked on a downtown sidewalk
by their recipient have been called out.
These are the conditions of our times, you say,
stuffing ourselves with what's greenish,
filming quickly in a garden
whose foliage is nearly realistic.
Once, we faced each other.
Now the unused filaments grow limp in us each day.
What huge thing catapults through you
when alone on the edge of your bed
is sincerity, or a need allow its mineral clarity

to bloom out your eyes,
but you'd rather it didn't.
Theory of feeling will sling feeling back to you
so you can just think it.
I offer these compact shapes of affection and sadness
which the words affection and sadness do not convey.
Cancer's sincere, shit is, indigestion, resentment
is sincere, sweat, dogs, mint, rust,
certain friendships are utterly sincere, and genitals
are sincere, though a flower is indifferent.

FIND LOVE IN BROOKLYN NOW!

It's true, my bed's a thorny nest I never really
let anyone into. But right now I'm roses; so here's the floor (you're
welcome).   Listen—my window fan's on HI,
nobody'll hear a thing. Rain

flecks the dirty sill clean . . . so for a minute at least, picture
what we'd do, no furniture in the next room.
What? a stabbing pain? forget it—
I'll try to—I mean, would you mind

just saying the thing that makes me
forget who I am. Forget *me*—
What's *your* definition of a narcissist? (show photo of father)—
Do I look like him? O, can't we be someone elses

groping each other by slatted light? —No, it's the neighbor's
kitchen, always on. Soft white, energy saver.
So save it—for yourself. Imagine putting the tailspin
back into your pants. I wanted to   , and now don't

know how: which button
do I push—
Oh yes the floor. It howls against you and (sort of) I'm sorry but
everything's better hard (can't argue there)—and I promise

later I'll pick off the lint, & I don't do that
for just anyone. Please
believe I want you,
pussy willow, chocolate gold foil-coin,

don't ungive the fly you flashed. It's raining studs. I only need to
carefully breathe alone a few moments, count to
what, nine?
sharpen my pencils.

Outside, the trucks charging down Nostrand Ave. hallelujah faster
(As if!)—as if they are teaching me to believe
I could get somewhere
by their methods—

THE HOLE

Down in the hole where all the old
Barbies are thrown, half-dressed
with tangled hair. Where the coral
lipstick. The clothes you were told looked good
because they were in style. In the hole lives
the sound of cellophane tape, the sort that turns
caramel with age, wrapping paper unrolled
onto the floor, and the plain clean
squeak of mother's scissor blades. It hurts in the hole
with such a warm house, windows lit and the people
on the couch and the people on the floor and
also in the photos, younger versions
of them smiling except your uncle
who never smiled. Cigar smoke. TV
blaring sports in the hole. All the throbbing
pasts crowded into the singular
throbbing present. The excess of presents
torn open and instantly forgotten. Chucked right
down into the hole. Hole where all the gone
cats. Where dinner. Where a dishwasher
and carpeted basement. Where the aunts
wore gaudy rings. And the full dinner plate not
by accident dropped on the floor. Hot food
jumbled in with shards of plate. Don't
you goddamn dare. The stomping up
or down the stairs. Snow and ice
and anyway nowhere to go. Sometimes the hole
a trick hole. Was that your old

name? the ring of the kitchen phone
with cord so long it grazed the floor? Their talk drifts up
when you aren't on guard so you swear
down into the hole as hard as you can
you'll never sit at their table again. When you yell
everything in the hole swims up so close
you smell the wine on its breath. The starched tablecloth
embroidered by relatives long-dead, the hands
refusing to release you even
after grace has ended.

STILL HERE

When you're in love the world appears more beautiful is something
people like to say. For me the heart's throat
is choked. Someone went in & scrawled a mustache
on the upper lip, and then
one under each eye.

There's the flood, the dam you have to keep
rebuilding. Who was driving? I didn't remember being
the passenger; we switched?   —it's understandable;
                                        I almost drove us off the bridge.

Or as if rotating on an axis and thrust into light
it's like this: I want us to be alone
but here's the world again that glows and strikes. I admit
I do want love to swallow us whole
and have us stay alive somehow in the being-swallowed & then not
be swallowed forever; we can come up for air,
and then we come up new and wise.

But it's true, his arm is so heavy sometimes
I can't breathe. The difference is
I'm not bothered, some other place breathes for me: I become
light and fast as music. And now I don't want to ever live
without that. (The mind always goes to *without that*.
Then the other thought: You'll be fine.)

But these days I'm not fine: love takes its big Sharpie
and draws mustaches on everything

which is to say it is everywhere reminding me of it and
laughing at me and sometimes I'm laughing too but mostly
stuttering a longing a doubting is a very difficult feeling
to maintain with the mustaches
like little dancing birds everywhere and my eyes so tired

                   And no balm exists or it does but it never
                   lasts long enough because then morning—

The only thing that stops the mustaches is the original mustache
belonging to the one shot through with this my stuttering my
    stumble

Except one thing.
I did see the disco ball, two beefed-up guys on Bowery
lifted out of the truckbed carefully.
One of them held it up waist-high and every
surface around them trembled with flecks of light.
The corrugated metal of the storefront gate, clutch of red
plastic grocery bags
in a woman's hands,
the austere stone entrance to the bank. Little white
ripplings, the world mirroring itself back. Saying *Hello. Here we are
we're still here.* And I walked through.

summer rain, a gasoline smell, almost mustardy, the unending pleasure flies seem to take in circling, the grey sky, how it's edged in odd distant clouds, cars idling at the stoplight, their impatient honking, a rolled-down window with dancehall bumping out, the determination of taxis, rain that comes suddenly and suddenly ends, sparrows sheltering under a broad-leafed tree, an intimate conversation held in public, wet sidewalk, whether or not to buy flip-flops made in China (are any flip-flops not made in China?), so many plastics, a woman in curlers hurrying down the street, her hair ruined, the tipped-over trash can, the rusted bicycle chained to the fence, someone speeding, the argument over a parking spot, the frayed rosebush, the varieties of other insistent flowers, the smell of garbage, a plane chalking its way across a swatch of sky, the mobile police surveillance tower parked around the corner over a week now, how its presence begins to seem normal, a dirty welcome mat, ceaseless hammering, an elderly man very formally dressed, the metallic tapping of his cane as he passes, the sky slowly clearing, but clearing to what, because blue isn't clear it's blue, two guys each holding a basketball, one guy with groceries, one with his mother walking slowly, a very bright yellow cloud, the neighbor who made signs for a living, who died but signs of him live all up the block, Custom Signs Here, No Parking Thank You!, Active Driveway, Divorce $250, Have It At MY PLACE, rain again trembling the leaves, the birds still huddling, a cat eating leftovers then shitting in the neighbor's potted plant, a car alarm, a bird whose song mimics a car alarm, oil stains on the road as on a favorite shirt, spattered, faint, but noticeable if you know where, how, why to look.

VOLLEY

In the absence of sunlight,
in the absence of a genuine river,
I blew air into a balloon. I gave my breath over
to its empty shape. I filled & pinched
& no matter how fast I tied it off,
how tight & swift, the air, my own, drained out.
And here I was again and here you were.
Watching? No, imagining.
So think what this balloon might represent
if we passed it back and forth
and took turns adding our breath.
What the quick tying might.
And our marveling at its lovely shape,
like an egg but also a tear-drop.
Our hands on it, our fingerprints
darkening its surface all powdery
and matte at first, with a bare sheen.
Think of the balloon sent into a crowd at a party.
How that crowd might move
to keep it in the air, protective
and playful, almost flirting with itself, a crowd
with light volleys will send & resend
a balloon upwards, high above their heads.
Until it drifts down
and asks to be touched by them again.
And with such innocent gestures, they do.
Though eventually they too will tire of this.
I can't just say *innocent*; I know that.

But I'm going to say innocent.
Innocent as a balloon
not meant to last.
Think of it handed
back and forth between us.

HORIZONTAL

From where I sit, four rectangles admit huge light
off the harbor, it burns tall, far upwards, the light
so blinding I take in and wish could
erase me seems a blessed escape from what and how I see
seeking voltage I notice an outlet's sad eyes
find faces in the water stains on my ceiling
in the table's wood grain the rumpled bedclothes
I must be terrifically lonely hallucinating
why now why this when there's so much else
to be wracked or unsettled by, but some essential
part of my intelligence dulls lately, minor heartbreaks
of the daily variety coalescing to gargantuan sorrow
that obliterates my finer powers of perception
do you also have oppositional drives the way I
want clamorous howling and dead quiet at once
to run as fast as possible burrow down under blankets
slow and geologic to shatter to mosaic be silk ripped in half
fucked till faceless cast into the outer galaxies then put back
together again? Right now the big door's thrown open
the storm door shut this dazzling light passes through its glass
I'm so afraid of knowing what I already know
and can't stop realizing how alone I am, we are,
then instant embarrassment at that thought
no revelation I'm just obsessed by it paining us all,
anytime I've approached feeling unalone
with someone anxiety overtakes me the person's
crowding body its breathing presence a suffocation and there's

no answer since anytime I've ever wanted to get inside really
knowing a person wanted them inside me
was when that couldn't be
and if it could I bolted or appeared to stand still
while actually vacating my body. I need to stop thinking
someone will appear in the doorframe silhouetted
extending their hand, I'm the one who has to build
from scratch the presence or the hand
must be my own, the person welcoming me
to whatever place I'm headed is all of ours where
do you see yourself going I mean long from now
where will you want to have been bound? There are islands
in the Chesapeake underwater today where last month
people sat on couches watching TV. Where the sky ends
the water begins and where in that should we?

RECOGNITION IS THE MISRECOGNITION
YOU CAN BEAR

Mostly a name feels like the crappy overhang I huddle under
while rain skims the front of me.

I admit it keeps me visible, the cool compromise
of efficient lighting, the agreement to call *this* that.

I follow the coil of a compact fluorescent
back to its root, inside a fixture
that imitates the moon

suitably enough, a For Rent sign hung in a window
where anyone might come to rest.

Alone on the avenues in open air I'm totally
outside myself, the coat but also
the thing inside the coat going around unseen,

unsure how I appear and whether
this constitutes a psychic problem
or simply the human condition.

Think of the interior of a lake,
almost entirely unavailable. Think of all
one face can transmit to another.

Mine looks far worse backwards than I imagine
it does when you see it for me,

the two me's shining back
from the wildlife of your one.

Still, I refuse to miss when a warmer light flattered us,
and the world burned out at alarming speed
while we brightened

at the sound of a bell, or hungered, pulling through
our respective mazes, not seeing them
for the variations on the same floor plan they were.

I still prefer the views from yours,
and to call the nowhere
most things come out of "The Blue."

Now I'm standing at the edge of this lake
Ohlone fished then white settlers turned
into a sewer. Settlers who fouled then moved

to clean it up as though to also own
the lake's rescue from ourselves
was a virtue. Volunteers in orange vests
sift out trash today with nets. My reflection

stares back from the refuse
crowded near its shore: a bobbing 5-Hour Energy,
two pair of jeans flattened
against lake's bottom, a sodden pillow

heavy with dreams I take uneasy
refuge in the facelessness of.

The empty water bottles and the dirty water
that are and aren't each other.

VARIOUS ATTENTIONS ALL LANDING LIKE BIRDS INTO THE SAME TREE AND THRILLING THERE SOME MINUTES AT DUSK

If I were a man, this would all be different—
        but I *"am"* a man—
                                        (a *"man"*)

Oh, stop harping
(how many women fuss over you—)

In the dream when he takes off his shirt, the outside of his body
looks like the inside. He's an artist (an *Artist*)—

                so is *this* what I need to learn how to do?

Wrestle down *"I"* with *"we"*
Then wrestle down *"we"* — (still hold dear
                experience & consciousness   as lived by an each)

Cast off and mock *"I"* like out-of-style clothes
        so now,
        what to wear, what to wear . . .

                (but *to feel*   fiercely)

Stop harping— *"I"* got sold and trademark'd by enemies
Excuse we, how speak?

There's a thin line of flame runs the length of each, mind to gut
                                find it & tie it to a crowd

If saddle up willingness plus experience what
can we make for us?

                              "we" turns a key

Voluminous we drop our coffees at once put our hands in the air

            How many utopias?   (keep imagining us)

Air gushing through a wide-open window
                                   the awe the branches belong to

DOT DOT DOT

Touch me lightly as we walk around the polluted lake.

Touch your arm to mine.

See the sunset behind the courthouse, and how they are one

institution touching another. To my elbow touch your own

as the pelicans dip their otherworldly faces

in unison into the night water. Starched dress shirts

without bodies in them, without heads.

Walk with me up the residential hill and down the other side.

As we sit across from each other at the unexceptional Thai restaurant

touch your leg to my leg. The table wobbles and because I am with you

I forget it. At the streetcorner,

smell the eucalyptus reminiscent of cat piss.

Glance with me into the cardboard box at the discarded khakis

and rollerboard suitcase, and touch my shoulder. This is the key

broken off inside my car door in desperation by a stranger.

Climb in through the trunk with me and touch your head to my head

at the cheek, at the temple, at the eye, at the lips.

Let's go to the mucky shore and watch

the gondolier in the striped shirt, a cliché and real,

stroking the water seriously.

Take my body away from me

lightly by touching me, take away

my head. Steer me with gentleness

from the sizeable heap of oranges molding at the curb

which I would otherwise describe further.

NO MORE BIRDS

Enough birds.
No more branches, no more moon, no more
clouds, light glinting on
no more water. Refuse to sing because
the song is stuffed and birds
they lilt and carol wordlessly of what, of whose
turn it is to bird and bird and bird
the same translations as assigned.
Whose turn is it to open-throated sing?
And what world's turn is it
to be sung of, a thing made noticed
that isn't, its beauty insisted. Who called again
to say what's ugly? Who pointed
from the other side of town, and which
frayed hem of a chainlink fence
did they mean. Did they mean
to suggest or outright say
is distinctly unbeautiful. This face?
The hand that cups it
or refuses to? The bodies
we inherited and tried to slip out of by pressing
pressing them together
together into finest dust? In which these little
dun intelligences do chip and flit. Do we, ought we
to care? For one another, yes.
Come here and crouch with me
at the unremarkable front stoop
of this medium-sized aspen tree

on an unnamed side of town.
Listen to their chattering or shrill world-songs
about our plastics and forgetfulness and bombs,
bombs of much unnumbered rubble, bombs of the reasonable
fear of bombs, dividing the living
from the living, towns from towns, constant speaking
or lip-synching with feathers
over the sound of the erosion of
whose turn it is to listen. Listen,
time to quiet down, beauty. Time to world.

ACKNOWLEDGMENTS

Thank you to the editors of the following publications, where earlier versions of these poems first appeared: *The American Poetry Review, Big Big Wednesday, DIAGRAM, Drunken Boat, The Feminist Wire, Guernica, Gulf Coast, LARB Quarterly, Love Among the Ruins, MiPOesias, Oversound, PEN Poetry Series, Pinwheel, Ploughshares, Poem-a-Day, Poetry Northwest, Portable Boog Reader 3, Southern Indiana Review, Spiral Orb, Subtropics, Sycamore Review, Tikkun, Transom, The Volta/Evening Will Come.*

Versions of these poems also appeared in the following: *Collective Brightness: LGBTIQ Poets on Faith, Religion, and Spirituality* (ed. Kevin Simmonds, Sibling Rivalry Press); *Testing Some Beliefs* (Gregg Bordowitz, If I Can't Dance, I Don't Want to Be Part of Your Revolution); *Troubling the Line: Trans and Genderqueer Poetry and Poetics* (ed. Trace Peterson and TC Tolbert, Nightboat Books); and the chapbook *What's Personal is Being Here With All of You* (Portable Press @ Yo-Yo Labs). Thank you to the editors.

Thank you to the Fine Arts Work Center in Provincetown, the New York Foundation for the Arts, the Wisconsin Institute for Creative Writing, the Bread Loaf Writers' Conference, Djerassi Resident Artists Program, Headlands Center for the Arts, Caldera, Campbell Corner, the Wallace Stegner Fellowship Program at Stanford, and Hunter College. For being a home I kept returning to while I wrote this book, gratitude to Unnameable Books.

Thank you to Wilder Alison, Jarrod Beck, Eavan Boland, Gregg Bordowitz, Ana Božičević, Kerry Carnahan, Sara Cooper, Liz

Countryman, Alina del Pino, Valentine Freeman, Suzanne Gardinier, Sara Gelston, Brenda Iijima, Amaud Johnson, Tennessee Jones, Jan Heller Levi, Candice Lin, Casey Llewellyn, Donna Masini, Miller Oberman, Hannah Oberman-Breindel, David Rivard, Margaret Ross, Tom Sleigh, Brandon Som, Sara Jane Stoner, Adam Tobin, Danica Varos, Stephanie Viola, Ellen Bryant Voigt, Anna Martine Whitehead, Sasha Wortzel, and all the friendships and conversations that have sustained me and these poems.

Enormous thanks to my editor, Jill Bialosky, for her belief in this book.

To keen & stalwart loves Cooper Sabatino, Solmaz Sharif, Aleksei Wagner—for seeing it, seeing through it, and seeing it through with me—radiant gratitude.

For being my parents always: my parents. I love you.

NOTES

"On Pockets" was inspired by Nicholas des Cognets and Michael Peterson.

"Gay Bars" is sourced entirely from names of gay bars in the continental U.S., some of which are no longer in operation.

"Recognition Is the Misrecognition You Can Bear" takes its title from Lauren Berlant's *Cruel Optimism* (Duke University Press, 2011).